The Colours of the South Downs

Glyn Kraemer-Johnson

Capital Transport

Acknowledgements

The author would like to thank all those who have provided photographs for this publication, with special thanks to Michael Eyre for his restoration work on many of them. Thanks must also go to those who have provided or checked factual information, especially Richard Maryon who has frequently abandoned a meal to delve into his archives for answers to my questions.

First published 2010

ISBN 978-1-85414-335-8

Published by Capital Transport Publishing
www.capitaltransport.com

Printed by 1010 Printing International Ltd

Contents

FRONT COVER
Guy Arab 544 turns onto Brighton sea front from West Street, a very busy corner, especially during the
time of the day-tripper as it was the route from the station to the beach. *Geoffrey Morant*

BACK COVER
The Bristol KS or KSW with highbridge ECW body was the standard Brighton Hove & District bus
throughout the 1950s, more than eighty being taken into stock. No.489 is seen in Richmond Place working
service 26, originally a Brighton Corporation trolleybus service that was extended to Mile Oak in 1961.
Roy Marshall

Introduction

'Sun, sand, sea and sangria' may be the synonym for today's holidays in Tenerife and Lanzarote but back in the forties and fifties it was more likely to have been 'Sun, sand, Sussex and Southdown'. It was a time when not only did people take their two-week annual holidays – and they were only two weeks – in the UK, but also when every Saturday, Sunday and Bank Holiday would see a constant procession of coaches from London and the Home Counties heading for the Sussex seaside resorts. The annual outing for many, whether it was factory, Sunday School or social club, was still 'a trip to the seaside on the chara'.

There is little doubt that memories of holidays and day excursions to the Sussex coastal resorts, of trips to Beachy Head and Devil's Dyke aboard open-top Guys or Mystery Tours in a Leyland PS1 or Tiger Cub all helped to put Southdown Motor Services Ltd amongst the most respected and fondly-remembered British bus operators. As too, for those of us brought up in the Southdown area, have memories of journeys to school, to meet the first girlfriend or to our first job. But there is more to it than that. It was Southdown's quality of service that really made it stand out from the rest.

The south-east of England was not noted for its independent operators; indeed these were few and far between. However, there were four major undertakings that operated within the Southdown area. The nationalised Brighton Hove & District Omnibus Company had been formed from the Brighton branch of Thomas Tilling Ltd and in the early post-war years had been remarkably innovative in its bodybuilding activities, giving many a pre-war vehicle a new lease of life. By the late fifties, like all the nationalised companies, the Bristol–ECW combination reigned supreme in the BH&D fleet although most managed to retain a certain individuality that set them apart from the other Tilling-Group operators.

Then there were the municipalities of Brighton and Eastbourne. Portsmouth has also been included in this volume because of its close ties with Southdown. Portsmouth had built up a large fleet of trolleybuses with low seating capacites and a high standard of comfort. In 1963 it followed the national trend and abandoned this silent and environmentally-friendly form of transport in favour of the motorbus. The City's Transport Department had always favoured Leylands and this continued until its privatisation and subsequent sale.

For the second and final stage of its trolleybus replacement programme, Brighton Corporation purchased fifteen Leyland PD2/37s with forward entrance Weymann bodies. Although with origins very definitely in the Orion design, they somehow managed to look much more attractive than their rear-entrance predecessors. Showing Brighton Corporation's policy of receiving maximum revenue from advertising, number 6 is seen in Grand Parade on former trolleybus route 42. *Alan Snatt*

4

Brighton Corporation began operating tramcars in 1901 but replaced them in 1939 with a mixture of motor and trolleybuses, all of AEC/Weymann manufacture. In the same year the agreement was reached with Brighton Hove & District to co-ordinate services in the Brighton and Hove area. A stipulation of the agreement was that the two operators should use the same red and cream livery, destination screen layout and fleetname. However, the Corporation buses carried the Borough crest beneath the fleetname and could also usually be identified by the incredible amount of advertising carried! The trolleybuses were finally abandoned in 1961, being replaced by Leyland PD2 motor buses. In the same year a new agreement was reached with both BH&D and Southdown from when the fleetname was changed to 'Brighton Corporation' although the red and cream livery was to be retained for several years.

Eastbourne Corporation had had the distinction of being the first municipal operator of motor buses when operations commenced in 1903. It had never operated trams. Before the war its vehicles were all petrol-engined, as the residents of this refined seaside town did not wish to have their peace destroyed by the clatter of the diesel engine. Chassis were fairly evenly divided between AEC and Leyland (plus a handful of Crossleys) while East Lancashire Coachbuilders generally supplied the bodywork. Eastbourne had class, and for many years even the advertisements were painted onto buses in fleet colours.

The distinctive crimson and white of Portsmouth, the smart red and cream of the Brighton operators and the beautiful rich blue, primrose and white of Eastbourne all contrasted well with the superb apple green and cream of Southdown and all added to the colours of the South Downs.

Glyn Kraemer-Johnson
Hailsham
East Sussex
March 2010

Having standardised on the AEC Regent V for a number of years, Eastbourne turned to the Leyland PD2 in 1966 for what were to be its last front-engined double-deckers. The Corporation continued to specify East Lancs bodywork, but that on the PD2s was to a more severe and less attractive design than that on the Regents. Number 81 is seen passing a Leyland Panther at Eastbourne station. Sister bus 82 was retained by the company, passing to Stagecoach with the sale of Eastbourne Buses in 2008. *Alan Snatt*

SOUTHDOWN

A ride on a Southdown bus was something special. Prior to 1961 Southdown charged higher fares within the Brighton area to deter short-distance passengers and thus protect the local operators. However, for many years I, and probably many others, thought the higher fares were payable for the privilege of travelling on a superior vehicle. A similar scheme had operated in Portsmouth until a co-ordination agreement was introduced in the city in 1946.

Internally, brown was the colour. Seat backs and cushions were covered in moquette of varying shades of brown and orange trimmed with brown leather whilst window surrounds were either dark varnished wood or half-brown, half-cream rexine in London RT style. Ceilings were deep cream. Some said the décor was drab but to me it shouted quality.

And then there were heaters; luxury indeed! Initially these were huge round affairs with chromium-plated surrounds and wire-mesh grilles that were fixed to the front lower-deck bulk-head. They were later replaced by heater units positioned beneath the seats that would whirr into life when the bus moved off and would die again when it came to rest. The only way to feel any benefit was to sit in the seat immediately behind with one's feet firmly against the mesh of the heater grille. Nevertheless at least there were heaters and it was to be the end of the fifties or early sixties before such indulgences appeared on BH&D and Brighton Corporation buses.

The Southdown livery, originally designed for Worthing Motor Services, one of Southdown's founder companies, was a stroke of genius. The apple green, dark green and cream fitted so well into the rolling Sussex downland through which the buses passed. Always pristine and immaculately maintained, the appearance of the vehicles gave rise to the epithet 'the Southdown Sparkle'. This was especially true of the Company's coaches, particularly those used on British or Continental holidays, which would depart with gleaming paintwork, crisp white antimacassars on every seat and not a dent or scratch to be seen. And this is how they would be maintained throughout the tour. Coaches played an important part in Southdown's activities but the scope of this book is confined to stage carriage operations so none are included.

At the end of World War II, apart from the utility Guys delivered from 1943 onwards, Southdown's double-deck fleet was composed entirely of pre-war Leyland Titans, many of which had suffered from poor maintenance throughout the war years. The company therefore embarked on a major rebodying programme, the bodybuilders involved being Beadle, East Lancs, Park Royal, Northern Counties and Saunders Engineering. Leyland TD5 227 had been delivered in 1939 with a 52-seat body by Park Royal. Just ten years later it received this new Beadle 54-seat body that almost looked older than the one it replaced! Beadle's post war bodies were of both six and five-bay construction, that on 227 being one of the latter. It was also one of a number of TDs to receive three-track route number boxes. The bus is seen at Worthing Pier while operating a local service. In the background is the Dome cinema and, behind the bus, the entrance to Southdown's Worthing garage and coach station. Note the crews, all wearing uniform caps. In those days incorrect dress was a serious offence. *Prince Marshall*

Then there was the fleetname. While most operators chose a fleetname style consisting of a large first and last letter with the intermediate ones underlined, Southdown chose ornate gold block capitals with black shading to the left and below. But this was only for service buses. Coaches carried the famous Mackenzie script fleetname, which at a glance suggested quality and class.

Southdown was not a particularly innovative company. It did not go in for new ideas or gimmicks. It introduced an ill-fated Leyland PD2/12 double-deck coach in 1950 that was tried on the Eastbourne to London express service. It was found to be grossly overweight and to roll alarmingly on corners and ended its days on school bus duties at Bognor. A 1948 Guy Arab and a couple of PD3s had experimental (and unsuccessful) heating and ventilation systems but apart from these the Company stuck with the tried and tested. In spite of this the vehicles themselves, whether buses or coaches, were always in some respect unique to Southdown. The Company set its own standards and specification for its 'cars' (Southdown's vehicles were never known as buses or coaches, always 'cars') and whatever the vehicle type the Company would somehow manage to stamp it with its own identity. Most vehicles had the chassis manufacturer's plate or badge removed and replaced with one that proudly proclaimed 'Southdown'. On underfloor-engined single-deckers and coaches this often meant that the chassis could only be identified by the wheel hubs. The Guy double-deckers were amongst the few that escaped this treatment.

The engine position was another area in which Southdown stubbornly held on to tradition. Neighbouring Maidstone & District had turned to the rear-engined Leyland Atlantean as early as 1959 but it was to be another ten years before the first examples entered the Southdown fleet, the company continuing to specify the Leyland PD3 until its last examples were received in 1967.

It was with the arrival of the first rear-engined buses that Southdown's tradition and individuality began to disappear. Three batches of Daimler Fleetlines with Northern Counties bodies, two of which entered service with the then recently absorbed Brighton Hove & District Company, maintained Southdown's high standard of comfort and interior specification but from then on it was all down hill. It was, of course, the time of the birth of the National Bus Company and it was not long before the splendid and much-loved apple green was replaced by a drab leaf green or, even worse in the case of coaches, all-over white.

Southdown as we knew it was dead.

Winters as they used to be! Another rebodied TD5, this time by Park Royal. The bus, probably 240, was delivered in July 1939, its original 52-seat body also being by Park Royal and was only eleven years old when it received the new 54-seat body shown here. The bus is working Brighton local service 111 and you can almost see it sliding down Bevendean Avenue on its way back to Old Steine. *Gerald Daniels*

In 1956/7 four Leyland TD5s dating from 1938 had their lives extended by being fitted with breakdown lorry bodies taken from earlier TDs. Seen in the entrance to Royal Parade garage, Eastbourne is 0198, which originally carried a Beadle 52-seat lowbridge body as bus number 198. On the left of the picture can be seen a preserved East Kent all-Leyland PD1. *Rob Crouch*

The ancient rescues the modern. In 1956/7 four Leyland TD5s had their lives extended by being fitted with breakdown lorry bodies taken from earlier TDs. Running on trade plates, one of the four is seen towing an all-Leyland PD2/12 past St Peter's Church, Brighton on its way to Edward Street garage. In this guise these former buses lasted in the fleet until the mid-seventies. *Howard Butler*

Amongst pre-war coaches remaining in the fleet was a number of Leyland Cubs with 20-seat Harrington bodies. The lives of many were extended due to the weak bridge connecting Hayling Island with the mainland. The Cubs were joined by Dennis Falcons and Southdown's only two Bedford OBs on services to and from the island. The weight restriction on Langstone Bridge was so severe that even these lightweight vehicles were unable to cross with a full load and a Park Royal bus-bodied Cub was stripped of all non-essential items and used as a shuttle bus to carry excess passengers across the bridge. A new bridge was opened in 1956 that allowed the use of normal full size vehicles. Harrington-bodied Cub number 38, dating from 1937, is seen at Havant Station on 26th August 1956, just a matter of weeks before its withdrawal. *Bruce Jenkins*

The Second World War brought with it the utility bus built to Ministry of Supply specification. The chosen chassis manufacturers were Guy Motors for double-deckers, single-deck production being allocated to Bedford. Bristol and Daimler were later added to the list and, as the war progressed, the specification became more relaxed. Southdown was lucky. It was allocated 100 Guy Arabs with 5- and 6-cylinder Gardner engines. It even managed to give all but eight of them registration numbers that matched their fleet numbers, something almost unheard of during the war years.

Six had extremely angular and ugly bodies by Strachans, but the rest were bodied by Northern Counties, Park Royal or Weymann. 429, seen here splashing through the rain in Portsmouth, was delivered in August 1944 and carried a Northern Counties 56-seat body, probably the most handsome of the four types having a deeper roof and more curvaceous domes. After the war, 429 was one of many utilities to be rebuilt by Southdown, being down-seated to 54, losing its opening front windows and having rear and side destination screens fitted, although by the time this photo was taken in May 1962, the side screen at least had been painted over. It also carried the simplified livery without dark green lining introduced in the late fifties. The bus was eventually withdrawn in 1964, having given a creditable twenty years' service. *Omnicolour*

The penultimate batch of utility Guys had bodies by Weymann. One such was 490 delivered in November 1945 and seen here in the entrance to Brighton's Edward Street bus garage. The bus remained virtually unchanged until its withdrawal in 1959. Note the metal sun visor, which was a characteristic of all Southdown buses of the period. Behind can be seen one of the East Lancs-bodied Leyland Royal Tigers in original condition with centre entrance. At the Brighton Hippodrome, John Hanson is appearing in 'The Student Prince'.
Prince Marshall

Below Having left the confines of the garage and moved into Edward Street itself, 490 shows off its quite pleasing rear end design. The original Ministry of Supply specification prohibited the use of curved panels resulting in the 'lobster-back' or 'stove-pipe' rear dome, made up of angled flat metal panels. By the time 490 was built in 1945 the specification had been relaxed considerably and allowed for a smoother, more rounded rear dome. In the late forties and early fifties the utility Guys were the mainstay of Brighton's local services to the outlying estates at Coldean, Bevendean and, in this case, East Moulsecoomb.
Prince Marshall

Between 1950 and 1959 many of the utility Guy Arabs were converted to permanent open-toppers to replace the ageing TD1s. There were variations in the conversions, the later ones having windscreens fitted to the front of the upper deck. 468 with Park Royal body was one of the earlier and arguably more attractive conversions dating from 1951, which lacked this addition. The bus is seen at the Beachy Head terminus of route 97 from Eastbourne. For many years the Traffic Commissioners had banned the use of double-deck vehicles on the Beachy Head route, resulting in Southdown's use of six-wheel Leyland Tiger single-deckers. By 1952 the restriction had been lifted and double-deckers were allowed to run to the top of the headland.
Omnicolour

Basking in the sunshine on Worthing sea front is 274, one of the first batch of Leyland double-deckers to be bought after the war. Whereas many chassis manufacturers continued to produce their pre-war models after the end of the Second World War, Leyland introduced new types for the bus and coach market. These were the PS1 (single-deck) and PD1 (double-deck) chassis, both of which used Leyland's new E181 engine developed during the war for use in military vehicles. Twenty-five PD1s were delivered to Southdown in 1946 with angular 54-seat Park Royal bodies that differed little from that manufacturer's final utility products as shown on the previous page. The 7.4 litres capacity of the E181 engine meant that the double-deckers in particular were very much under-powered, resulting in them spending much of their lives on the flatter routes in West Sussex although an impression of one of these buses climbing the steep hill out of Eastbourne on service 12 adorned the front of the Company's timetables for many years.
Prince Marshall

Mention has been made of the five utility Guys which were fitted with particularly austere and unattractive bodies by Strachans, two being of lowbridge layout. In 1951, all five received five year old East Lancs bodies taken from elderly Leyland TD2s. They spent most of their second lives working in the Worthing area. 406 - one of the few Southdown buses not to have matching fleet and registration numbers – belies its wartime origins as it circumnavigates the roundabout at Worthing Pier in 1959. *Martin Jenkins*

Southdown's second batch of Leyland PD1s arrived in 1947 and carried Leyland's own handsome metal framed body, a development of the pre-war product introduced in 1936 having a redesigned cab area. This was to form the basis of Leyland's double-deck bodies until its bodybuilding activities ceased in 1954. The all-Leyland PD1 could always be distinguished from the PD2 with the same body by the fact that the offside front mudguard did not protrude beyond the dash. Another characteristic of the PD1 was its slow tickover when idling, the whole bus shuddering with each surge of the engine as if it must surely stall. Services 9 (Brighton–Littlehampton) and 10 (Brighton–Arundel) were the regular haunts of these vehicles, again largely due to their flat terrain. 305 (HCD 905) turns from Steyne Gardens on to Worthing sea front while working the latter route. *Omnicolour*

In 1947 Leyland revised the Titan, fitting it with the 9.8 litre 0.600 engine, which had been used in goods vehicles since 1946 and which was to prove extremely reliable and long-lived. In fact the engine was to remain in production for some twenty-five years. The new model was designated, quite logically, PD2 and in 1948 Southdown took delivery of no fewer than 80 Leyland PD2/1s (316-395; JCD 16-95), again with Leyland's own bodywork. With its larger engine, the PD2 was much more powerful than its predecessor and the 'JCDs' became the mainstay of frontline services for several years. By the time this photograph was taken however, they had been demoted to less arduous duties such as Brighton local service 49, introduced as a result of the Brighton Area Transport Services (BATS) agreement in 1961. Under this agreement the operations of Southdown, Brighton Hove & District and Brighton Corporation were co-ordinated with receipts being pooled on a percentage basis. 374 rounds Old Steine, Brighton, passing a Brighton Corporation forward-entrance PD2 of much later vintage. *Rob Crouch*

14

Another route taken over by Southdown under the BATS agreement was the 15, which ran between Patcham and Upper Portslade, The route had been operated by Brighton Hove & District from the days of its predecessor, Thomas Tilling Ltd. This rear view of PD2/1 number 334 at the top of Ladies Mile Road in Patcham shows the bus with temporary black-on-white destination blinds. The S-shaped rain guttering over the rear upper deck window was a trademark of Leyland bodywork. The oval panel in the cream surround below the rear lower deck window housed the brake warning light: a red STOP illuminated on a neutral ground. In 1965 the Patcham Fawcett High School for Boys was built on the fields in the background. It lasted only until 1989 when it was demolished and replaced by a housing estate. *Howard Butler*

Below From Patcham, service 15 buses continued on route 13, travelling via Hollingbury and Old Boat Corner before descending into Coldean and thence to Pool Valley via Lewes Road. In this fine shot 326 is seen climbing Carden Avenue with the post-war Hollingbury estate in the background. *Howard Butler*

388 had spent much of its life operating from Bognor garage and latterly Brighton. In early 1967 it was transferred to Eastbourne and put to work on service 93. The reason? Road works at Jevington made it necessary for a vehicle narrower than the eight feet wide double-decker normally used and the 7ft 6ins wide PD2/1 fitted the bill admirably. It is seen leaving Terminus Road, Eastbourne for Wannock and Jevington. *Dave Brown*

Southdown routes 110 and 111 to Lower Bevendean linked at the terminus, thus performing a circle around the Bevendean estate. 333 passes 'Bevendean Shops' on its way to the terminus at Bodiam Avenue. The PD2/1s gave yeoman service, some not being withdrawn until 1967 after a creditable nineteen years. *Gerald Daniels*

Nearing the end of their days and looking rather the worse for wear, two all-Leyland PD2/1s (376 and 393) are seen at Portsmouth. Like most Southdown double-deckers delivered prior to 1958, these buses had originally carried dark green lining beneath the windows on both decks but the lining-out was abandoned in the mid-fifties to simplify painting. These two buses were amongst the last to be withdrawn in 1967. An Aldershot & District AEC Reliance lurks in the background. *Rob Crouch*

Presumably impressed by the rugged reliability of the utility Guys, Southdown supplemented its delivery of Leyland PD2s with twelve Guy Arab IIIs powered by Gardner 6LW engines delivered between October 1948 and July 1949. To peacetime standards, of course, they had bodies by Northern Counties to that bodybuilder's distinctive design of the time featuring heavily radiused top corners to the front upper deck windows, a characteristic of most Lancashire coachbuilders' contemporary products. They were mainly divided between Brighton and Portsmouth where they were usually to be found working local services although occasionally they would venture further afield. 508 was following the usual trend when photographed in Pool Valley waiting to depart on service 13 to Patcham. On the left is 757, a Leyland PD2/12 with a later version of the same body. *Howard Butler*

17

Many of Brighton's local services departed from Old Steine rather than the main Pool Valley bus station and this is where we see Guy Arab III 510 laying over between duties on the 109 service to East Moulsecoomb. 510 was one of a number of Southdown double-deckers to be fitted with translucent fibreglass panels in their roofs and these are clearly visible in this view. Whilst the upper deck was much lighter as a result of this modification, it was also a lot colder in winter. The bus had also gained an additional ventilator in the front dome. *Geoffrey Morant*

1950 saw the maximum permitted dimensions of double-deckers increased to 8ft x 27ft 6ins and Leyland increased the size of its PD2 chassis accordingly, Southdown's choice being the PD2/12 (with vacuum brakes). It also introduced a revised body design, known as the 'Farington', clearly derived from its predecessor and still a very handsome body. The PD2/12 was to become the mainstay of the Southdown fleet throughout the fifties and, apart from a solitary and rather unsuccessful double-deck coach bodied by Northern Counties, its first examples were twenty-four with Farington 58-seat bodies received in 1951. One such was 721 seen arriving in Brighton's Old Steine from Littlehampton and heading for the entrance to Pool Valley. *Rob Crouch*

There were eventually a total of fifty-four all-Leyland PD2/12s in the Southdown fleet and for many years they maintained front line services including the four-hour long service 31 from Brighton to Southsea. However in this view 730 (LUF 230) from the second batch is, despite the lack of a route number, operating on a 'short' working on service 12 to Seaford whilst the 1948 all-Leyland PD2/1 is about to depart on the marathon run along the Sussex coast and into Hampshire. The photo offers and interesting comparison in that 730 wears the original livery with dark green lining whilst PD2/1 356 has lost its lining but retains the cream area beneath the top deck windows. When the revised livery was finalised the apple green was taken up to the bottom of the windows as shown in the upper photograph.

The Leyland Royal Tiger was, hardly surprisingly, the choice of chassis for the first single-deck buses to be bought since before the war. These were ten PSU1/13s with rear-entrance bodies by East Lancs. They featured a vee-shaped dip in the cream waistband below the windscreen, something that was to characterise all but a handful of single-deckers right through to the introduction of the rear-engined chassis. In 1958/9 these buses were all converted to front-entrance for one-man operation and passengers lost that privileged opportunity to sit up front, next to the driver. 1501 passes Patcham Fountain and the Black Lion Hotel on a deserted A23. *Howard Butler*

The LUF-registered Royal Tigers, 1500-9, could initially be distinguished from their later brethren by the flat nearside windscreen. All had originally had dark green roofs but these were lost when liveries were simplified to aid economy. 1505 stands in the entrance to Petersfield Garage. The '1500s' were the mainstay of the single-deck fleet until 1967/8 when they gave way to 36ft long vehicles. *Gerald Daniels*

East Lancs-bodied Leyland Royal Tiger 1521. When new these vehicles had a full screen display on the back although this was later reduced to show route number only. On conversion to front entrance many of the 1500s were reseated to 41 whilst others received 39 seats, the extra space being occupied by a 'pramcontainer' luggage rack. While not unattractive from the front, the East Lancs body was otherwise quite dated with its high waistline and multitude of small windows. 1521 was one of a number of saloons to receive a script fleetname. The bus is waiting in Pool Valley, Brighton to depart for Chelwood Common on service 30. The 30/32/36 group of services to Chelwood Common, Uckfield and East Grinstead, together with the 21 to Shoreham Beach, were the preserves of the East Lancs Royal Tigers for many years. In fact until one man operation really took hold in the early sixties, they were among the very few single-deck routes to work out of Brighton. *Howard Butler*

The second batch of East Lancs-bodied Royal Tigers comprised thirty saloons numbered 1510-39. They differed from the initial batch in having centre rather than rear entrances but they too were converted to front-entrance to allow for one-man operation between 1959 and 1961. The 'MCD' 1500s originally had recessed nearside as well as offside windscreens but flat screens were fitted on the nearside when they were converted to front entrance, presumably to allow room for the doors to open. 1515 passes St Peter's Church in Brighton. *Gerald Daniels*

To help the acute shortage of new vehicles in the immediate post-war years, John C Beadle of Dartford, hit upon the idea of building 'new' integral coaches utilising the running units from life-expired pre-war AEC and Leyland chassis, most being supplied to BET Group companies. Fifty such vehicles were delivered to Southdown between 1952 and 1954, which used chassis parts from Leyland TS8 buses and coaches. The first twenty were built to the newly introduced maximum length of 30 feet and carried 35 passengers in their centre entrance bodies. The remaining thirty were unusual in being 26ft long with 26-seat front-entrance bodies. 874 was one of the latter and utilised the running units from 1442, a 1938 Leyland TS8. The 26-seaters were equally at home on rural bus services as private hire and excursion work and in 1957/8 many were converted for stage carriage work, although there was little outward evidence of the conversion; even the destination screens remained the same. They were renumbered at the same time; 874 became 651 and is seen at Chichester while working the Saturdays only service 164 to Oving. When this view was taken in May 1963, the vehicle still retained its dark green roof. *Southdown Enthusiasts' Club*

The two versions of Southdown's double-deck livery are evident in this view. Circumnavigating the roundabout by Worthing Pier, utility Guy 417 wears the simplified livery introduced in the late fifties. PD2/12 764, however, working the long 31 service from Brighton to Southsea via Portsmouth, still retains its dark green lining. Both vehicles have bodywork by Northern Counties. In the background, also with fully lined-out livery, is one of the all-Leyland PD2/1s operating a Worthing local service. *Prince Marshall*

As previously mentioned, the Brighton single-deck services were normally the province of the Royal Tigers and the appearance of the Tiger Cubs was not that common. On this occasion, however, 626 was waiting in Pool Valley ready to depart on service 32 for Hayward's Heath and Uckfield, usually worked by Royal Tigers. The temporary nature of its operation in Brighton is borne out by the fact that 626 was apparently not equipped with the correct set of destination blinds. These buses had an unusual mixture of sliding vents and 'Routemaster-style' quarter-drop windows and, while the moquette was of Southdown's standard pattern, the seats were not, having lower backs with curved top rails. *Howard Butler*

Alfriston, situated between the A27 and A259 north of Seaford, is popular with tourists, not only because of its picturesque nature and 'olde worlde' atmosphere, but because of the number of antiques shops in the village. It is also home to the 14th century Clergy House, the first property to be acquired by the National Trust. Tiger Cub 630 stands in a shady spot in the village square while working service 126 from Eastbourne to Seaford. This route still runs today but is now operated by an Optare Solo minibus on a County Council contract. 630 appears to have acquired an apple green front dome to its otherwise dark green roof. *Gerald Daniels*

In 1955 another twelve Leyland PD2/12 double-deckers were delivered, this time with 59-seat bodies by Park Royal to a design that obviously owed a lot to the London RT. Unlike the RT, however, and similar bodies supplied to most operators, the Southdown examples were of five-bay construction. To order – and receive – buses that were such a major departure from the bodybuilder's standard product showed just how much weight was attached to the Southdown name. When most operators had adopted the sliding vent, Southdown maintained its preference for the half-drop. Park Royal-bodied Leyland PD2/12 770 is seen entering Pool Valley bus station. Southdown seemed to have a propensity for bus stations and depots with difficult access. Eastbourne's Pevensey Road bus station and Brighton's Manchester Street Coach Station were cases in point, but none was more so than busy Pool Valley where buses had to swing out into the traffic of Old Steine in order to negotiate this narrow approach road. Some of the paving slabs were later removed to allow access for larger vehicles. On the right can be seen the entrance to the Enquiry Office, above which was the Cashier's Office where conductors would pay in their takings. *Howard Butler*

At the other end of the 38 route, Number 774 leans over as she turns from Bevendean Road into Eastbourne Road. The 38 route was renowned for its steep hills, tight timings and the number of gear-changes required on a round trip. This gave rise to it being known as 'the race track'. During its lifetime the route was worked by all three local operators at various times with an amazing variety of vehicles. Brighton Corporation used AEC Regent Is and IIIs, Brighton Hove & District Bristol Ks and Lodekkas while Southdown's offerings were Leyland PD2s, PD3s and Guy Arabs! *Howard Butler*

1955 saw the arrival of more Guy Arab double-deckers. These were twelve Guy Arab IVs with Park Royal bodies virtually identical to those on the 'OCD' PD2/12s and numbered 512-23. The first of the batch is seen here at the Golden Cross terminus of service 16 from Brighton. The terminus was almost in the middle of nowhere, being little more than a pub on the main A22 midway between East Hoathly and Hailsham. Southdown was renowned for its connecting services and, although the 16 could have been extended to Hailsham or Eastbourne, it terminated here and connected with the 92 from East Grinstead to Eastbourne on which passengers could complete their journey. No doubt Southdown saved a vehicle in the process. These buses, together with the Park Royal PD2s, were Southdown's last to feature half drop windows. *Howard Butler*

Park Royal was obviously the favoured bodybuilder of 1955 for five Leyland Tiger Cub 39-seat saloons also had bodies by this manufacturer. Numbered 640-44 they were at first glance, much the same as the Duple/Nudd Brothers version, but there were a number of differences. The rear side windows were longer, obviating the need for the rather fussy rearmost window of the Duple version, and the front corner pillars followed the slope of the windscreen making for a neater and more attractive appearance. 642 is seen on Worthing sea front while working local service 106, and appears to be moving away from the stop with the doors still open. *Roger Knight*

Following on from the OUF-registered Guy Arab IVs, Southdown took delivery of a further thirty-six in 1956. (More often than not the company seemed to order its vehicles in multiples of twelve.) These again had Park Royal bodies and were basically the same as the OUFs, although they seated 59, two more than the previous batch. The most noticeable difference, however, was that Southdown had at last abandoned its love of half-drop windows and specified sliding vents for these buses which, arguably, gave then a sleeker appearance. Here we see a busy scene at Horsham Carfax with Arab IV 533 showing 'Private' on its destination screen and, in the background, one of the earlier batch working service 17 to Brighton. Note on the right, the fine selection of British cars led by a rather bulbous Standard Vanguard. *Prince Marshall*

Taking a much slower turn into the Baden Road terminus of service 38 than the PD2 shown earlier at Bevendean Road is Guy Arab IV 527. The Park Royal Guys were used on the 38 for a while but their slow gear changes meant that they were not particularly suited to the route's tight schedules. The curtains of the house behind are drawn but no doubt the throb of the Gardner 6LW would have found its way into the bedroom! The steel foothold just left of the foglamp enabled the conductor to reach up to the destination blind winding handle beneath the canopy. *Gerald Daniels*

One can almost hear the whine of second gear and the beat of the Gardner 6LW as Guy Arab IV 549 pulls away from the traffic lights at St Peter's Church on the last lap of its journey to Pool Valley. Following an initial spell on the busy service 12 from Brighton to Eastbourne, for which they were not ideally suited, these handsome buses were for most of their lives the mainstay of many of the company's 'inland' routes, leaving the coastal services to the contemporaneous PD2s. 549 is apparently working the 117 from Horsham, although the destination blind is showing the intermediate points for service 23! The 117 was originally numbered 17 but was changed under the Brighton Area Transport Services Agreement to avoid confusion with BH&D's famous sea front service 17. *Howard Butler*

Crawley was one of the 'border' towns where Southdown buses met those of London Transport. Showing off its handsome lines, Guy Arab 554 is seen at what was then the Crawley Bus Station, whilst working local service 79. Following a reorganisation of services in the Crawley area in 1971 this route passed to London Country becoming its 479. Many enthusiasts will agree that the mid to late fifties saw bus design at its peak. This was certainly the case with Southdown whose Guy Arab IVs and Beadle and East Lancs-bodied Leyland PD2/12s represented what to many was the pinnacle of the British double-decker. Fortunately examples of all three types have survived into preservation and Park Royal-bodied Guy Arab 547 is frequently seen at rallies and running days, giving enthusiasts the opportunity to savour those wonderful sound effects and the almost sumptuous comfort of its interior. *Geoffrey Morant*

The next twelve double-deckers to arrive were very definitely unique to Southdown. They were Leyland PD2/12s with bodies by John C Beadle of Dartford. Beadle were supplying large numbers of coaches at the time but these were the first double-deckers to be built by the company for some years and, as it happened, were destined to be the last. They were built on Park Royal frames and were very similar to the Park Royal bodies on Guy Arabs 524-59. About to pass the exit from Pool Valley and with the clock tower of the Brighton Aquarium in the background is 785. Sister bus 786 was repatriated from France for preservation and has been magnificently restored to its original condition. *Geoffrey Morant*

Two services operated between Eastbourne and Hastings and both were operated jointly by Southdown and Maidstone & District. The 15 took the inland route via Hailsham, Herstmonceux and Ninfield while the 99 followed the coast road via Pevensey, both routes meeting at Bexhill. In this view Beadle-bodied PD2/12 783 is seen turning from Sea Road, Bexhill into de la Warr Parade ready for the last lap of its run into Hastings. Today both routes are still operated by Stagecoach, the 15 having been renumbered 98. *Rob Crouch*

Service 24 was originally a circular service from Brighton via Hurstpierpoint, Ditchling and Lewes, but the section between Lewes and Brighton was withdrawn, being amply covered by other services. Under a cloudless blue sky Beadle-bodied Leyland PD2 777 sweeps round Old Steine to its terminus at Pool Valley. A quartet of Brighton Hove & District Bristols can be seen in the background including, nearest the camera, a convertible Lodekka in cream livery and behind it, a KSW6G. Note the informative bus stop sign. *Rob Crouch*

Southdown's final PD2s were probably the finest. Twenty-four were delivered in 1956/7 with handsome 59-seat bodies by East Lancashire Coachbuilders featuring electrically operated sliding doors on their rear platforms. Their operation was quite simple but ingenious. The main portion of the door slid into a space behind the rear nearside seat while the lower left-hand 'quarter' was hinged, allowing it to move inwards behind the rear wheel. Their main problem was that when the bus was facing up a steep incline, the electric motor was insufficiently powerful to open the door smoothly. The result was that the door would either 'judder' open slowly and noisily, or refuse to open at all, which made these vehicles very unsuitable for the hilly service 38 on which they appeared occasionally! As well as the frontline coastal services 12 and 31, these buses were for many years to be found on the 119 service from Brighton to Tunbridge Wells and its sister, the four-hour long 122 to Gravesend, both of which were worked jointly with Maidstone & District. 808 is seen passing Sussex University at Falmer, on the outskirts of Brighton, with a very long way to go before it reaches its destination beside the Thames estuary. *Gerald Daniels*

Uckfield was the meeting point for a number of routes, including the 119 and 122. Heading home to Brighton is East Lancs PD2 807, a regular performer on the route. In the background is one of the first 36ft Leyland Leopards, identifiable by having a curved rear dome instead of the standard BET rear end that was to follow. 807's sliding door can be seen in the open position through the rear lower deck window. Southdown continued to specify five-bay construction for its half cab double-deckers until the end, although in the case of East Lancs it was still the coachbuilder's standard product and was to remain so until production of the front-engined chassis came to an end. *Dave Brown*

Much of the 122 route was very rural in nature, especially the section north of Tonbridge. 812, numerically the last PD2/12 to be purchased by Southdown and also the last rear entrance double-decker, is seen passing Shipbourne Common with St Giles Church in the background. 812 was withdrawn in 1971 and sold to Cope Allman Plastics in Portsmouth for staff transport. It ended its days somewhat ignominiously by losing its roof in a low bridge accident. *Dave Brown*

Borough Green Maidstone & District garage was the point at which crews would be changed, with a Maidstone & District driver taking the bus on to Gravesend. 812 is about to continue on its way northwards while sister bus 805 is on a Southdown Enthusiasts' Club tour. 805 was sold to Kenzie of Shepreth, Gilbert & Turner of Stanford-le-Hope and Avro of Corringham. It was then purchased for preservation and is fortunately still with us today. *Rob Crouch*

Journey's end. 810 at Overcliff, Gravesend already well laden for the 50 mile-long return journey to Brighton. Behind is a Maidstone & District Weymann-bodied Bristol K6A together with a couple of single deckers, probably AEC Reliances. *Howard Butler*

On 1st July 1956 the maximum permitted length for double-deckers was increased to 30ft and all the major manufacturers responded by introducing lengthened versions of their existing chassis. Leyland was no exception and the PD2 became the PD3 in thirty-foot form. Southdown took delivery of its first PD3s in 1958 and had them fitted with forward entrance Northern Counties 69-seat bodies, little realising how many would enter the fleet over the next nine years, or how much of an icon the type would become, almost rivalling the London Routemaster in popularity. The design of body was used on half-cab double-deckers supplied to Wigan Corporation but, apart from a few rebodied and rebuilt buses, the full-front version was unique to Southdown. It is interesting to study how the basic design developed over the years. As illustrated by 820 (TCD 820), the initial batch had sliding vents on all side windows and the front upper deck windows had the characteristic Northern Counties radiused top corners. Old Steine, Brighton is the location. *Rob Crouch*

After the absorption of the Brighton Hove & District Company, many PD3s were drafted in to replace the Bristol Ks, being given Southdown–BH&D fleetnames. One such was 836 photographed on former BH&D service 19. This bus had only a year of its life with Southdown remaining but still had that 'Southdown sparkle'. Because of their increased length they were given the nickname of 'Queen Mary', a name that has been synonymous with them ever since. Along with 820 and 830, 836 was one of many PD3s sold to the China Motor Bus Company in Hong Kong for further service where they were reunited with a large number of former Southdown Guy Arab IVs. *Roger Knight*

The third batch of PD3s arrived in 1959/60 and were fitted with opening front vents on the upper deck, considerably altering and modernising the original design and taking away some of its 'droopy' appearance. Southdown's most westerly services, the 45 group of routes that operated between Portsmouth and Fareham, had been the first to receive 30ft double-deckers when the 'TCD' batch had been allocated to the services in 1958. By the time this photograph was taken at Fareham Bus Station, 852 was working on the 45A to Southsea. *Howard Butler*

The old Brighton to Kemp Town railway line crossed Lewes Road on a high viaduct, always known as 'Lewes Road Arches' from where this impressive photograph was taken. Far below (the photographer obviously didn't suffer from vertigo!) we see one of the 28xx CD-registered Queen Marys on Brighton local service 13, being pursued by a Marshall-bodied Leyland Leopard that has made its way from Chailey via Lewes. The imposing red brick building in the centre background is the offices and garage of what was then Brighton Corporation Transport. It started life in 1901 as a tram depot, later housing the Corporation's fleet of trolleybuses. It continued to serve as the main depot in the days of Brighton Blue Buses and is still in use by the Corporation's successor, the Brighton & Hove Bus and Coach Company. The large modern building in the background was, at the time, the Brighton College of Technology and now forms part of Brighton University while the road on which the PD3 is travelling is now one way and part of the 'Vogue Gyratory System'. *Roger Knight*

Although outwardly similar, the next PD3s, delivered over the winter of 1961/62, were mechanically very different. They were of type PD3/5 and were fitted with pneumo-cyclic semi-automatic gearboxes. They were not a success and, much like the PD1s before them, most found their way onto the company's flatter routes, mainly in West Sussex. They did work on the long route 31 to Southsea, although this itself was fairly devoid of hills. However, 914 is seen on Worthing sea front while operating on one of the more usual routes, Worthing local service 7. All forty of these buses were fitted with illuminated offside advertisement panels, another innovation that was not particularly successful. *Omnicolour*

Another advertising innovation of the time was the overall advert. This had been tried in London but Southdown was the first provincial company to have a vehicle painted in this way. The bus chosen was 915, one of the PD3/5s and the advertiser was Roberts Off Licences. As can be seen from this photo of 915 in Pool Valley, the bus was basically orange and decorated with bunches of grapes and bottles of wine. Other all-over adverts followed, some quite tasteful, others hideous. The practice continues to this day although nowadays the front of the vehicle is usually painted in fleet livery to avoid confusion to the public. *Dave Brown*

A final batch of Leyland Tiger Cub saloons arrived in 1961, this time with rather plain bodies by Marshall to the basic BET Federation design of the time. The vee-shaped moulding below the windscreen was the only concession to Southdown's hitherto standard specification. Ten of these buses were taken into stock and 655 is seen in Pool Valley waiting to depart on railway replacement route 80. Rather surprisingly they lasted for only ten years in the fleet, most subsequently passing to Wimpy, the building contractor. *Howard Butler*

Southdown's first 36ft single-deckers were twenty-five Leyland Leopards with Marshall 51-seat bodies. The bodies were something of an interim product, being basically to the standard BET Federation design but, while the front end featured the double-curvature windscreen and peaked dome, a curved rear dome was retained, giving the buses a rather old-fashioned appearance when viewed from behind. They were down-seated to 45 on conversion for one-man operation and the entire batch of twenty-five was sold to East Kent in 1971. When first introduced these buses were used as crew-operated vehicles, as shown by the conductor standing beside the driver on 683 as it descends Uckfield High Street on its way from East Grinstead to Eastbourne. There is no longer a through service between these two towns, passengers being required to change buses at Uckfield. *Omnicolour*

The second batch of Leyland Leopard single-deck buses were also bodied by Marshall but to standard BET Federation design, the only concession to Southdown being the traditional vee-shaped dip in the moulding beneath the windscreen. Twenty were delivered in 1963 as 51-seaters but like their predecessors, had their seating capacity reduced to 45 on conversion to one-man operation. While the Leopard saloons were widely used to convert former double-deck routes to o.m.o, 106 is seen leaving Brighton with a respectable load on service 30 for Chelwood Common, which was always a single-deck route. *Rob Crouch*

After its fairly unhappy experience with the forty PD3/5s, Southdown returned to the PD3/4 with synchromesh gearboxes for its next and all subsequent deliveries of Titan double-deckers. However, the twenty-five with reversed 'CUF' registrations delivered in 1964 were, like their predecessors, equipped with illuminated offside advertisement panels, although Commercial Union Insurance and Wavy Line grocers were amongst the few national advertisers to take advantage of this innovation, many buses carrying Southdown's own publicity. Bruford's the Jewellers of Eastbourne was one of the few local advertisers to make use of illuminated adverts, as illustrated by 967 pictured here pulling out of Brighton Station forecourt on the busy service 12 to Eastbourne. This batch of PD3s was also the first to be fitted with dual headlights, which seemed to tidy up their frontal appearance somewhat.
Alan Snatt

By 1964 the open-top utility Guys were past their prime and so in that year Southdown took delivery of a further twenty-five PD3/4s with the usual Northern Counties bodywork, but with removable roofs for use on the company's seasonal open-top routes. One of the most popular services was that from Eastbourne to the top of Beachy Head. This had always been Southdown's preserve, Eastbourne Corporation vehicles having to terminate at the 'Foot of Beachy Head'. With a full top-deck load of passengers enjoying the sea breezes, 402 makes its way westward along Eastbourne sea front. *Geoffrey Morant*

While the 97 terminated at the top of Beachy Head, the 197 continued to Birling Gap and East Dean before returning to Eastbourne via Old Town. An unidentified PD3 is seen passing Birling Gap with the chalk cliffs of Beachy Head and the lighthouse in the background. *Omnicolour*

With their 'lids' on, the convertible PD3s could always be easily identified by the slightly shallower roof and the heavy ribbing below the upper-deck windows. Identification was made easier still later in their lives when they were all given a 'one-eyed' look, having donated a front opening vent to the Panoramic PD3s of 1967. This shot was taken in the days when hospital visiting was restricted to half an hour in the evening and two hours on Wednesday and Sunday afternoons. Southdown operated services from outlying areas to various hospitals within its area and convertible PD3 420 was working to Summersdale Hospital near Chichester when this picture was taken. *Rob Crouch*

The 1965 delivery of Northern Counties-bodied PD3s, with BUF–C registrations, probably saw the Queen Mary at its best. Internally they had dark wood-grained Formica side panels and seat backs and featured an attractive moquette in various shades of green and fawn. There were forty in all, the last five being convertibles. 283 waits at Old Steine before setting off on the 112 circular service to Brighton Station and West Dene, returning via London Road. The 112 interworked with the 12 group of services, buses continuing from Pool Valley to Rottingdean, Saltdean and beyond.
Rob Crouch

One of this batch, 257 differed considerably from the rest in having an automatic heating and ventilation system, the radiator being installed beneath the stairs. As a result the seating capacity was reduced to 65 instead of the usual 69. The arrangement also made it possible for a standard double-curvature windscreen to be fitted which, in the writer's opinion at least, improved its appearance. The bus was not a resounding success and seemed to spend most of its life working on services 9 and 10, home of unloved buses! Note the mixture of sliding and Rotavent windows in this view of 257 laying over in Pool Valley.
Roger Knight

Single-deckers continued to be Leyland Leopards with BET Federation-style bodies. The 1966 intake consisted of twenty with 45-seat bodies by Weymann and were, in fact, amongst the last to be built by that firm at its Addlestone factory. Basically the same as the Marshall examples, they were noteworthy for their sparsity of opening windows. 143 is seen in Seaside, Eastbourne nearing the end of its long journey from East Grinstead.
Geoffrey Morant

A further thirty Northern Counties-bodied Leyland PD3/4s were delivered in 1966 numbered 285-314 with corresponding FCD-D registrations. Basically the same as the preceding batch, the most noticeable difference was the fitting of Auster 'Rotavent' windows. In simple terms these consisted of a plastic tube inside a metal casing. Both parts had in them long slots which, when lined up, allowed fresh air to be drawn into the vehicle. Only two per side were fitted on each deck although the buses retained their 'push-out' vents at the front. 296 hurries along the coast road through Saltdean towards Brighton with the Saltdean Lido in the background. *Howard Butler*

One more 'D'-registered PD3 arrived in October 1966 although it was officially part of the 1967 order. The reason for its early appearance was that it had been exhibited by Northern Counties at the 1966 Commercial Motor Show. It bore little resemblance to the standard Queen Mary although it was in some ways a development of 257, having a similar heating and ventilation system mounted beneath the stairs, which again allowed for a double-curvature windscreen with straight lower edge to be fitted. The main body structure however, was more akin to that currently being supplied by Northern Counties on rear-engined chassis. A fixed 'wrap-around' windscreen was fitted to the front of the upper deck and the bus featured extra-long side windows, there being just three per side on the upper deck and two on the lower. Car 315 was registered GUF 250D and was a rare example of a Southdown bus with non-matching fleet and registration numbers. It was photographed when new while operating a Southdown Enthusiasts' Club tour. *Rob Crouch*

Delivery of the final batch of PD3s, and indeed of Southdown's last front-engined double-deckers, began in January 1967. They had conventional radiators and the standard Queen Mary front windscreen arrangement although the cream paint below the lower deck windows was taken straight across the front instead of following the curve of the windscreen. Otherwise the bodies followed the pattern set by 315 with wrap-around upper-deck windscreen and long side windows, which led to them being known as the 'panoramic PD3s'. They retained the curved rear lower-deck side windows that had been standard on all PD3s but which looked particularly archaic on the panoramics. As with 315, ventilation was provided by Auster Rotavents. 369 was photographed when still fairly new, ably demonstrating that 'Southdown Sparkle' as, with Brighton's Palace Pier in the background, it heads eastwards to Rottingdean, Saltdean and the quaintly named Peacehaven Annexe. The banners on the roundabout are promoting the annual Brighton Festival. *Rob Crouch*

The influx of 36ft Leyland Leopard single-deckers continued unabated to aid the extension of one-man operation. One batch of fifteen was bodied by Willowbrook to the usual BET Federation design but made easily identifiable by lacking the traditional Southdown vee-shaped moulding beneath the windscreen. Most however had bodies by Marshall, such as this 1967 example. By this time the all-invasive Rotavents had spread to single-deckers as shown by 170 approaching Pool Valley with blinds already set for the return journey to Eastbourne. Behind is Brighton Corporation Leyland Atlantean number 90 in all-over advertising livery for Barclaycard. *Dave Brown*

Following nationalisation in 1948 the products of Eastern Coach Works and chassis manufacturer Bristol Commercial Vehicles (formerly part of the Bristol Tramways and Carriage Co.) had only been available to companies within the state-owned Tilling Group in England and Wales and the Scottish Bus Group north of the border. However in 1965 the Leyland Motor Corporation purchased a 25% share in both ECW and Bristol after which it was possible for both concerns to offer their products on the open market. Prior to its nationalisation the Bristol chassis, noted for its rugged reliability, had been a popular choice with a number of municipalities and some BET concerns including North Western and Southdown's neighbour, Maidstone & District. Southdown itself, primarily a Leyland stronghold, had never operated the type and it caused quite a stir, therefore, when in 1967 a total of forty Bristol RE single-deckers entered the fleet. Not only were they the first Bristols for Southdown, they were also the first rear-engined vehicles to be operated. The Bristol RE was offered in two lengths and Southdown's were of the shorter (33ft) RESL type. They were powered by the Gardner 6HLW engine, a horizontal version of that fitted to the majority of Guy Arabs and carried Marshall 45-seat bodies which, although to the standard BET design as fitted to Southdown's Leopards, had their appearance altered considerably by the fitting of a front-mounted radiator grille required by the RE. This also meant that the characteristic vee-shaped moulding was no longer possible. Car 248 is seen 'resting' between duties in John Street, Brighton. *Alan Snatt*

This was a time when the rear-engined single-decker was being seen as the answer to the bus operators' prayers and all the major manufacturers introduced models to this layout. Leyland had the Panther and its offspring the Panther Cub, AEC designed the Swift and Merlin, large numbers of which were bought by London Transport only to be sold on within a short space of time, and Daimler launched its Roadliner, renowned for its unreliability. None was truly successful with the exception of the Bristol RE, many of which proved to be long-lived. Most of the rear-engined chassis had a step to the raised rear section above the engine and rear wheels whereas the RE had a gently ramped floor that was step-free. Obviously happy

with its first examples, Southdown took delivery of a further twenty REs in 1969, this time of the 36ft RELL type. Again they were powered by the trusty Gardner 6HLW and had bodies by Marshall, this time with seats for 49 passengers. They also heralded the end of the Auster Rotavent, being fitted with 'hopper' type windows that considerably improved their appearance. 435 is seen in Crawley Bus Station working a relief duty on service 79, a circular route running between Crawley and Gossops Green. In the early seventies, following a reorganisation of services in the area, it passed to London Country Bus Services, becoming their 479. *Gerald Daniels*

1st January 1969 saw the birth of the National Bus Company and with it came a rationalisation of bus companies and their areas throughout England and Wales. As a result the Brighton Hove & District Omnibus Company, formerly a Tilling Group concern, became part of Southdown from that date. At the time BH&D had on order two batches of ten Bristol VRTs, that manufacturer's first rear-engined double-decker. The first ten were delivered direct to Southdown between February and April 1969 in full BH&D red and cream livery, the only clue to their new ownership being the registration numbers which, in accordance with Southdown tradition, were issued by Brighton Borough Council. BH&D buses had always been registered in East Sussex. These buses introduced one-man double-decker operation to the Company. They entered service on BH&D service 8 and later replaced Bristol REs on the 43/44 group of services. Initially numbered in the BH&D series as 93-102, they subsequently had 2000 added to their fleet numbers. 2098 is waiting to turn into Elm Grove with, in front, a Southdown Harrington-bodied Commer and, bringing up the rear, a Morris 1000 police Panda car. Another VR is descending Elm Grove on route 44. *Roger Knight*

The third batch of vehicles to be delivered in 1969 arrived in the autumn. They were unusual and quite probably unique to Southdown. Based on the usual Leyland Leopard chassis, they had 49-seat bodies by Northern Counties to dual-purpose specification. Livery was apple green with a dark green waistband and they were exceptionally high with steep entrance steps, a strange choice for bus work when companies were turning to rear-engined chassis with a step-free entrance. They were used mainly on stage carriage work when the front offside seat was converted to a luggage pen, reducing the seating capacity to 47. Number 455 is seen leaving Eastbourne Bus Station on the comparatively short service 199 to Pevensey Bay on which its dual purpose seating was probably appreciated, though hardly essential. *Alan Snatt*

Quite a stir was caused at the beginning of 1970 when ten 33ft Daimler Fleetlines with Gardner 6LX engines were delivered for the former Brighton Hove & District fleet. They had Northern Counties 71-seat dual-door bodies and were painted in full BH&D livery (albeit with red rather than black wheels). Internally, however, they were to Southdown's usual specification with the company's standard seats and moquette together with wood-grain Formica on seat backs and side panels. The unusually low seating capacity for vehicles of their size meant that there was ample legroom and, indeed, they introduced a new standard of comfort to the passengers used to travelling on the Bristol KSWs they replaced. The body design was a natural progression of that on the Panoramic PD3s with double-curvature windscreen, wrap-around upper deck windscreen and panoramic side windows, the appearance being improved by the vehicles' extra length. 2103 was the first of the batch and is seen in the company of two similar buses, outside the former Brighton Hove & District garage at Conway Street, Hove. *Dave Brown*

Bearing in mind Southdown's long association with Leyland one might have expected it to turn to the Atlantean for its rear engined double-deckers, but the Fleetline was definitely the preferred choice. There followed a further fifteen, again with Northern Counties bodywork, but these were of single-door layout and only 30 feet in length. Unfortunately their appearance suffered as had that of the Panoramic PD3s; they were not really long enough to take the larger windows and consequently ended up with a rather 'dumpy' look. By the time they were delivered the era of BET's Southdown was drawing to a close but the 'Southdown sparkle' remained. 377 was in pristine condition when photographed working a Worthing local service. *Alan Snatt*

In October 1970 a further ten Bristol RESLs were received with Marshall 45-seat bodies. They differed from previous REs however in having Leyland 0.680 engines, which made them very lively performers. A number were allocated to Brighton's busy route 38 where they coped admirably with the hills, traffic and tight schedules. However, 481 is seen working on circular service 112. One can almost hear the throbbing exhaust as it crests the hill at Fiveways, Ditchling Road and prepares to turn into Preston Drove. Not its normal route, but the photograph was taken on the day of the Brighton Carnival when services had been diverted away from the Preston Park area. *Roger Knight*

Six more Bristol REs were to be delivered to Southdown, all with standard ECW bodies. Three, received in the autumn of 1970, were dual-door Gardner-engined RESLs for the BH&D fleet. Two were painted red and cream, the third being in Southdown livery although this too was repainted red and cream before entering service. March 1971 saw the arrival of the second trio, which were of the longer RELL type with Leyland 0.680 engines and 50-seat ECW bodies. These were to be the last REs for Southdown, the type being supplanted by the Leyland National in 1973. These three saloons spent most of their working lives on Brighton local services. 601 is seen nearing Old Steine at the end of its journey from the Woodingdean estate on the eastern outskirts of the town. The bus lane in Grand Parade in which 601 is travelling was subsequently removed only to be returned to use some years later! *Dave Brown*

Southdown continued to receive ECW-bodied Bristol VRTs and was to do so until 1981, the type being the National Bus Company's standard double-decker. However, in the autumn of 1971 a further fifteen 33ft Daimler Fleetlines were received with dual-door Northern Counties bodies and were painted in the red and cream of the former Brighton Hove & District company. Basically similar to the previous batch, the main difference was the power unit, these buses being fitted with the Leyland 0.680 engine. Again they had the standard Southdown interior but, perhaps a little strangely, had Tilling-style moquette instead of the usual Southdown green. Externally they could be distinguished by the absence of an opening vent on the foremost upper-deck side windows and by the single central ventilator in the front dome. 2127 was the last of the batch and the very last bus to be delivered in BH&D livery. It also differed from its fellows in having a fully automatic gearbox. Unfortunately it was one of a number of vehicles, including 2117 and 2121 from the same batch, that were totally destroyed by a disastrous fire in the former BH&D Conway Street garage on 14th April 1978. It is seen here in happier days when new and looking absolutely resplendent in its red and cream livery as it waits at Old Steine to depart on the circuitous service 54 to Hangleton. *Dave Brown*

The following spring saw the arrival of another fifteen Fleetlines, again with Leyland 0.680 engines, but to the shorter 30ft length and with single door Eastern Coach Works bodies, basically to the same design as that used for the VR. They were the last buses to be delivered in the traditional apple green and primrose livery that had graced the company's buses for some fifty-seven years. They marked the end of an era and the end of Southdown as we knew it. For the next decade or so, with the exception of two batches of Leyland Atlanteans, the Bristol VR and Leyland National reigned supreme as did the National Bus Company's uninspiring leaf green and white livery. The penultimate true Southdown bus 398 arrives in Old Steine at the end of its short journey from Bevendean on Brighton local service 111. This entire batch of Fleetlines was sold to Crosville Motor Services in 1984. *Dave Brown*

What more appropriate way to end this section than with this rear view of the iconic Southdown Queen Mary, in this case 864 and one of the final buses to be delivered in Southdown livery, Daimler Fleetline 397, photographed at Old Steine and both working former Brighton Hove & District routes. *Dave Brown*

PORTSMOUTH CORPORATION

Like many municipal operators Portsmouth Corporation, or the City of Portsmouth Passenger Transport Department to give its full and rather grandiose title, had commenced its operations with trams. These were later supplemented by a small fleet of motor buses but in 1934 a start was made on replacing the trams with trolleybuses. Trolleybuses of a variety of makes were purchased for evaluation purposes, but the fleet was mainly of AEC and later BUT manufacture. When it came to motor buses, however, Portsmouth was very much a Leyland stronghold. The first Leylands, seven TD1s and a solitary Lion, had been delivered in 1931 and the manufacturer remained the major supplier of vehicles until the privatisation and sale of the undertaking in 1988. Other makes did enter the fleet, but this was often due to necessity rather than choice.

Portsmouth's wartime allocation of utility vehicles included, somewhat unusually, ten Bedford OWB single-deckers, eight with 32-seat bodies by Duple and two by Mulliner. For utility buses they were fairly long-lived and in 1958 were used to introduce one-man operation to the corporation, subsequently surviving into the early sixties. One of the Duple bodied examples, number 169, is seen in 1959 looking immaculate. It was one of the last to be withdrawn, and by the time it left the fleet in 1963 it had clocked up a very creditable nineteen years of service. *Roy Marshall*

From the first TD1s delivered in 1931 Leyland became Portsmouth Corporation's favoured chassis manufacturer. More TD1s were delivered in 1932 followed by twelve TD2s in 1933. Both types had bodies by English Electric. In 1935 the TD4 was the choice with sixteen being delivered that year. Numbered 115-30, the first twelve had English Electric bodywork, the remaining four being bodied by Leyland itself. In 1953 four of the English Electric-bodied TD4s were rebuilt as open-toppers to inaugurate a sea front service. In this condition they continued in service until 1971 by which time they were an incredible thirty-six years old. Number 8, previously numbered 125, is seen on Southsea sea front shortly before its withdrawal. Happily this bus is still with us. Following a spell in the Portsmouth Museum, it now resides in the Milestone Museum at Basingstoke. *Dave Brown*

As might have been expected with its Naval dockyard, the city suffered badly during World War II. Ten Corporation buses were destroyed by enemy action and the depot at North End was damaged. To compensate, nineteen utility buses were allocated to the fleet comprising ten Bedford OWB single-deckers and nine Daimler CWA6 AEC-engined double-deckers. Interestingly in 1958 the Bedfords were modified to become the undertaking's first one-man operated buses. Peacetime saw a return to Leyland although thirty-four Crossley double-deckers were delivered during 1948/9. In the immediate post-war period operators were clamouring for new buses to replace war-damaged and time-expired vehicles and, while bus production continued apace, it was very much a case of buying what was available. This could have been the case with Portsmouth's Crossleys although the Department had operated a number of Crossley Condors in pre-war days.

In July 1946 Portsmouth Area Joint Transport Services came into being which brought about the co-ordination of all Portsmouth Corporation and Southdown services within an area bounded by Fareham in the west, Petersfield to the north and Emsworth in the east. Although Corporation vehicles rarely ran as far as the boundaries, the CPPTD was able to introduce services well beyond the city limits into what had previously been solely Southdown territory. Thus the crimson and white buses reached as far as Paulsgrove and Portchester in the west and the growing satellite town of Leigh Park in the east where, unusually, the two operators shared a garage.

Following extensive trials with a variety of chassis types the AEC 661T was chosen as the standard pre-war Portsmouth trolleybus. Two batches were delivered, the first in 1935 consisting of nine AEC 661Ts with English Electric 50-seat bodies. Like Southdown, Portsmouth believed in offering its passengers comfort, hence the low seating capacity. The second batch of no fewer than seventy-six trolleybuses arrived during 1936/7, again on AEC 661T chassis, but with bodies by Cravens of Sheffield seating 52, still unusually low. Being overtaken by an Austin A55 Cambridge in this 1961 view is Cravens-bodied AEC 249, formerly numbered 49. It is seen at The Hard about to depart for Eastney with a similar vehicle behind. Travelling in the opposite direction is one of the all-Leyland PD2/10 motor buses. The Hard, also known as 'Dockyard', was a very busy trolleybus terminus, hence the three rows of overhead wires. *Marcus Eavis*

The final trolleybuses for Portsmouth, received in 1950/51, were based on 9611T chassis built by BUT, the joint enterprise formed by AEC and Leyland for the production of trolleybuses. Their curvaceous bodies were by H V Burlingham of Blackpool and again seated just 52. A very definite holiday atmosphere pervades this view of number 315 at Southsea Common on route 6 in 1961. Portsmouth had an unusual route numbering method. Trolleybus services were numbered while motor bus routes were lettered. Moreover, different numbers were used for different directions of travel, thus number 315 on its return journey would carry route number 5. In the background can be seen one of Portsmouth's utility Daimler CWA6s that had received a new body by Crossley in 1955. Just two years after this photo was taken Portsmouth finally said goodbye to its trolleybuses. Fortunately one of these fine vehicles, number 313, is in the safe hands of the East Anglia Transport Museum at Carlton Colville and has recently been fully restored. *Marcus Eavis*

Like Southdown, Portsmouth Corporation bought Leyland PD1s, twenty-five arriving during 1947/8; actually a mixture of PD1 and PD1A types, the latter having Metalastik rubber bushes instead of metal as on the standard PD1. Six had 52-seat bodies by local coachbuilder Reading, although whether this was through a desire to support local industry or the necessity for quick delivery is not clear. The bodies on these buses were wooden-framed using unseasoned wood and proved troublesome throughout their lives. The remaining nineteen, with a mixture of DRV and DTP registrations, had elegant bodies by Weymann and were to prove longer-lived, the last not being withdrawn until 1967. Number 193 became the Corporation's driver trainer in which guise it is seen here. *Malcolm Keeley*

Crossley chassis were not common in the south of England, although some were operated by Eastbourne, Luton and Reading. The Crossley body was even more of a rarity. In 1949 Portsmouth took delivery of 25 Crossley-bodied DD42/TTs, which were known as 'Gearless' buses, having an early form of automatic transmission. Both engines and transmission proved extremely troublesome and they were eventually replaced with engines and gearboxes removed from withdrawn Leyland TD4s. Number 57, the last of the batch, waits to start its run to Fratton Park, Portsmouth Football Club's home ground. These were the days when it was still common practice to rent a television set. *Howard Butler*

This fine 1960 nearside view of Crossley DD42 number 48 illustrates the characteristic lines of the Crossley body as well as the unusual front mudguards favoured by the manufacturer. With all windows open on what is obviously a hot summer's day, the bus also shows off to perfection Portsmouth's beautiful lined-out livery. In the background is one of the all-Leyland PD2/10s. *Marcus Eavis*

1952 saw a return to Leylands with the delivery of 25 PD2/10s with Leyland's own handsome 'Farington'-style bodies. They were very similar to Southdown's Leyland-bodied PD2/12s but were only 7ft 6ins wide. Again like Southdown, Portsmouth continued to specify half-drop windows long after most operators had turned to the sliding ventilator. Number 68 heads for Southsea's South Parade Pier. *Howard Butler*

With less than a year to go before its withdrawal, PD2/10 number 65 is beginning to show signs of wear and tear but nonetheless still looks like a thoroughbred as it deputises for an open-topper on the Sea Front service. Some of these buses put in a very creditable nineteen years service with the City Transport Department. *Roy Marshall*

Above The Metro-Cammell Orion was not the most attractive of bodies with its frameless domes and unequal depth windows. The Portsmouth examples on Leyland PD2/12 chassis differed from the standard Orion by having winding half-drop windows, unusual on this type of body, and the window pans had much squarer corners than was usual. Portsmouth's superb livery of crimson and white with yellow lining-out also helped their appearance considerably. A total of forty of these buses were delivered to Portsmouth in 1956 and 1958, some of which were later converted to open-toppers. Number 88 lays over beside a particularly informative bus stop at the Canoe Lake, Southsea. *Dave Brown*

Opposite page top One-man operation had been introduced by Portsmouth Corporation in 1958 using the wartime Bedford OWBs, suitably modified. 1959 saw the arrival of ten Leyland Tiger Cubs with dual-door Weymann bodies offering seating for 34 passengers and standing room for a further 16. They were unusual in that the centre doors opened when a passenger trod on the step. Negotiations with drivers over pay for one-man operation delayed their entry into service until 1960 when they were used to convert two routes to o.m.o, these being the services from Highbury to Wymering and Hilsea to Paulsgrove. Number 21 with Tiger Cub badge proudly displayed, heads for Clarence Pier passing a pair of proud parents pushing a 'proper' pram. *Howard Butler*

Opposite page bottom 1968 and the trolleybuses have gone, but The Hard interchange is as busy as ever with a fine array of Corporation vehicles all of Leyland manufacture. Taking centre stage is Tiger Cub 146, which is working former trolleybus route 17 to Eastney. Note that Portsmouth was still using its ornate gold fleet numbers at this time, at least on the fronts of its buses. *Roy Marshall*

Thirty-one years of bus design are spanned in this view taken in September 1967 at South Parade Pier. On the left is English Electric-bodied Leyland TD4 number 5, originally numbered 115 and new in 1935. Along with three of its contemporaries it was converted to open top configuration in 1953, in which form it remained in service until 1971. All four of the buses survive in preservation. On the right, contrasting sharply, is Leyland Atlantean 249 of 1966; more advanced, no doubt, but lacking the character of its pre-war counterpart. It too became an open topper, being converted in 1978. *Roy Marshall*

Between 1963 and 1966 the MCW-bodied Leyland Atlantean PDR1 was the standard Portsmouth double-decker. 246, seen at South Parade Pier, Southsea in September 1968, was one of the final batch delivered in 1966. A number of these buses were converted to open-top, many being given extended lives by sightseeing tour operators throughout the country. 246 retained its roof, however, and was withdrawn from service in 1980. Something a little odd appears to have happened with the paintwork at the rear of the lower deck! *Roy Marshall*

BRIGHTON HOVE & DISTRICT

BH&D had been a leader in the introduction of open-top seaside services, their route 17 from Rottingdean to Portslade having been introduced as early as 1936 using Tilling 'ST-type' AEC Regents dating from 1930 that had been fitted with new purpose-built open top bodies. By the mid-fifties the AECs were past their prime and were replaced by 1940 Bristol K5Gs with ECW bodies that were rebuilt as convertible open-toppers by the operator. The conversion was particularly thorough. The bonnet was lowered and the post-war PV2 radiator fitted. The bodies were completely rebuilt, featuring 'standee' windows on the lower deck and the result was some very attractive vehicles that belied their age – although it has to be admitted that with the roof in place they looked a little odd. So successful was the 'Sea Front Service' during the fifties that in 1955 six K5Gs built between 1938 and 1941 were purchased from the then Bristol Tramways company and converted in the same manner, although only two were convertibles, the others becoming permanent open-toppers. Showing just how attractive the resultant vehicles were is number 994, the oldest of the former Bristol vehicles dating from 1938 (second-hand vehicles in the BH&D fleet were numbered backwards from 999). It is seen with a healthy top deck load passing the exit from Pool Valley where a Southdown PD3 is basking in the sunshine.
Howard Butler

The Brighton Hove & District Omnibus Company Ltd was formed in November 1935 from the Brighton and Hove section of Thomas Tilling Ltd and it followed therefore that it should become a Tilling Group company. On its formation the fleet consisted mainly of Tilling ST-type AEC double-deckers, the same as those operated by Tilling in London. The first Bristols arrived in the fleet in 1936 after which, apart from two final AECs, a couple of Dennis single-deckers and two utility Guys, all future motor buses were of this make.

In 1939 agreement was reached with Brighton Corporation (which was replacing its trams with motor and trolleybuses) under which services in the town were co-ordinated with mileage and revenue being pooled on a percentage basis. The agreement also specified that the fleet-name 'Brighton Hove & District Transport' should be used by both operators and that livery and destination screen layout should be common to both. It was also agreed that BH&D should operate one-fifth of the trolleybus network, which led to it becoming the only Tilling-group company to run trolleybuses. Eight Weymann-bodied AECs were delivered in 1939 although they did not enter service until after the war. Three BUTs, also with Weymann bodies, arrived in 1947. The trolleybuses were basically the same as those being operated by the Corporation, although there were detail differences, especially internally.

For its size of around 150 buses, the company's bodybuilding activities were quite remarkable and innovative. Indeed many of the Tilling AECs had had their original bodies built at the Company's coachworks in Holland Road, Hove. Unfortunately the building was destroyed by fire in 1945 and bodybuilding activities were subsequently carried out at the Conway Street garage. At the end of World War II the BH&D fleet still had a fairly high AEC content, many dating from the early 1930s and, like Southdown, the Company embarked on a massive rebuilding and rebodying programme. Beadle of Dartford and Eastern Coach Works were

Brighton Hove & District had the distinction of being the only Tilling Group company to operate trolleybuses, something that came about by the 1939 agreement with Brighton Corporation, which required the company to operate 20% of the trolleybuses. Eleven trolleybuses were operated in all, eight AEC 661Ts and three BUT 9611Ts, all with Weymann bodywork. Basically similar to the Corporation's vehicles, there were detail differences such as flush fitting destination boxes contrasting with the protruding ones of the Corporation's trolleys. The first eight were delivered in 1939 but were stored until after the War. The only route operated solely by BH&D was the 44 from Seven Dials to Black Rock, which crossed over Brighton Racecourse. On Race Days grass was laid on the roadway, the road being closed. As a result service 44 buses terminated at the Race Hill whilst a shuttle service was operated from the other side of the racecourse to Black Rock. 344 was one of the 1939 AECs and is seen outside the Company's Arundel Road garage, a building still in use today by BH&D's successor, the Brighton & Hove Bus & Coach Company. Note the semaphore traffic indicator that has characteristically not returned home. The trolleybuses were the only BH&D buses to have this type of indicator. *Geoffrey Morant*

responsible for most of the new bodies built, but BH&D itself carried out extensive rebuilding work, especially to the Tilling ST types, which still had open staircases. The company also built three complete bodies, one of which was the first bus in the country to be fitted with fluorescent lighting. Unfortunately this was in the days before the transistor and the experiment was not a success. In addition there were a large number of body changes between vehicles that made the time a fascinating one for the enthusiast, even though keeping track of the various body movements was something of a complicated task. During the fifties the bodyshop was very much engaged in the rebuilding of pre-war Bristols to convertible open-top form. Unlike many operators this was not simply a case of removing the roof but involved a total rebuild, even to lowering the radiator and bonnet line.

The first Bristol K had entered the fleet in 1937 and was to remain the standard vehicle until it ceased production in 1957, when the company purchased the last one to be built. From 1959 the Lodekka became the mainstay of the fleet. However, the very last vehicles to be delivered to the true Brighton Hove & District company were ten Bristol RESLs, the first single-deckers to be bought for nearly thirty years.

The 1939 agreement was replaced in 1961 by the Brighton Area Transport Services (BATS) agreement, which saw the co-ordination of services, including those of Southdown, within an area extending from Telscombe in the east, Falmer and Pyecombe to the north and Shoreham in the west. This brought about a major reorganisation of services and took BH&D buses to such places as Saltdean and Shoreham Beach, hitherto the sole preserves of Southdown.

On the formation of the National Bus Company, BH&D was absorbed by Southdown. The red and cream livery lingered on for a while, Southdown apple green and cream replacing it for a while before both fleets received NBC corporate leaf green and white.

The wartime allocation of utility vehicles to Brighton Hove & District had consisted of two Guy Arabs with rare Pickering bodies and ten Bristol K6As with bodies by Park Royal. In 1946 the first Bristol Ks were delivered with ECW's immediate post-war 56-seater highbridge body (very similar to that which had been used to rebody many of the pre-war AECs) and this became the standard vehicle. Forty were taken into stock between 1946 and 1950 fitted with either the six-cylinder Bristol AVW engine or the Gardner 5LW unit. 387 was one of the K6Bs delivered in 1948 and is seen at the Mackie Avenue terminus of service 5B. Apart from being more powerful, the Bristol AVW-engined vehicles gave a much smoother ride than their Gardner 5LW counterparts. The litter bin in the picture appears to have been designed for children – and small children at that! *Howard Butler*

The BH&D trolleybuses were withdrawn on 24th March 1959 at the first stage of the abandonment scheme. For just over a month, until the arrival of the first Bristol Lodekka on 28th April, the fleet was composed entirely of Bristol K-types. Apart from the final eight, which were of 7ft 6ins width, the 8ft wide highbridge KSW had been the standard choice since 1952, the fleet now containing more than sixty of the type. And it was no surprise that they should take over from the trolleybuses. Although standard Tilling Group issue, since 1954 the BH&D Ks had been fitted with Beatonson 'Rapide' combined sliding and hopper ventilators that required the fitting of a metal louvre above the side windows that gave the buses a very distinctive if rather severe appearance. 476 was the last of the first batch to be so equipped and is seen here on service 44A, a slight variation of trolleybus route 44. Clearly visible is the white steering wheel denoting that the bus was eight feet wide. *Gerald Daniels*

Pool Valley had always been the sacred preserve of Southdown's vehicles, apart from a few Maidstone & District buses on jointly worked routes. At any rate it had always been green. However, the introduction of the Brighton Area Transport Services agreement in 1961 saw the red and cream buses of Brighton Hove & District entering the hallowed surroundings for the first time. The 38 route, referred to in preceding pictures, had in its BH&D and Corporation days terminated at the bottom of West Street outside the SS Brighton Ice Rink. This had involved vehicles performing a U-turn that, as traffic had increased, had become more and more difficult – and dangerous. In 1962 therefore the route was extended to Pool Valley. Seen laying over in Pool Valley is BH&D 497, one of a batch of eight 7ft 6ins wide Bristol KS6Gs, the final one of which, number 500, was the very last Bristol K-type to be built. Next to 497 is Southdown Northern Counties-bodied PD2/12 759 on service 9, which followed the inland route via North Lancing to Worthing and Littlehampton. On the far left is a Maidstone & District AEC Regent V with Park Royal body on one of the jointly operated services into Kent. *Howard Butler*

Left Brighton Hove & District was the last Tilling-Group company to order the Bristol Lodekka, as it had no services that required low height vehicles. But, having purchased the last Bristol K-type to be built in 1957, it no longer had a choice. The first Lodekkas arrived in 1959 and by 1967 no fewer than 92 were in service, two thirds of the entire fleet. The first eight to arrive were officially classified as LDS, in effect being prototypes for the flat-floor FS-type that was to follow. They featured air suspension and were fitted with the Cave-Brown-Cave heating system, which in theory obviated the need for a traditional radiator. Thus, when delivered the buses had a plain front cowl decorated with a Bristol winged motif. However, overheating problems resulted in them being fitted with the customary radiator grille. They started a new numbering system from 1. Numbers 4-8 (OPN 804-8) were closed top buses in standard red and cream and were put to work on the busy 38 route. Numbers 1-3 were convertible open-toppers and were therefore painted in the Company's cream and black open-top livery. They were also the last buses to be fitted with the standard BH&D destination screens although these were subsequently reduced to show route number and ultimate destination only. With roof firmly in position OPN 803, by this time numbered 2003 in the Southdown series, waits at the Hollingbury terminus of services 46/46B. *Dave Brown*

Below left The most numerous Lodekka type was the 27ft 6ins rear entrance FS but in 1961/2 fifteen of the rarer FSF types were purchased. These were again 27ft 6ins 60-seaters but with forward entrances. The first and last five were powered by Bristol's own BVW engine but the middle five, numbered 31-5, were the first BH&D Lodekkas to be fitted with the Gardner 6LW. They also featured illuminated offside advert panels. One such was 33 seen here breasting the top of Braybon Avenue with the Patcham estate spread out below in the background. The 46 service on which the bus is working had originally been a Brighton Corporation trolleybus route, those vehicles making short work of the steep gradient. 33 would have made slower progress! As can be seen the trolleybus traction poles are still in place and in use as lamp standards. *Howard Butler*

Above The final and possibly the finest Lodekkas delivered to BH&D were 30ft forward entrance FLFs fitted with the more powerful Gardner 6LX engine. Twenty of these handsome buses were taken into stock between 1965 and 1967 although eight were later transferred to the Scottish Bus Group in exchange for rather dubious 33ft Bristol VRs. Looking superb in its traditional BH&D red and cream, KPM 83E lays over in the sunshine at Old Steine. By this time it had gained Southdown's 2000 prefix to its original fleet number. *Dave Brown*

It had hitherto seemed unlikely that BH&D and Southdown would ever be taking delivery of the same vehicles at the same time, but that is what happened in July 1968, at least as far as the chassis were concerned. These were the last buses delivered new to Brighton Hove & District, and its first single-deckers for some thirty years. They were fitted with ECW dual door 37-seat bodies with a central area for standing passengers, the latter quickly earning them the title of 'cattle trucks'. They were used initially to convert services 8 and 44 to one-man operation but later settled down on service 37 from Southwick to Kemp Town. Under Southdown ownership they migrated westwards to Portsmouth. Numerically the penultimate BH&D vehicle, 209, by now numbered 2209 in the Southdown fleet, passes through Old Steine on its usual working. *Roy Marshall*

BRIGHTON CORPORATION

Brighton Corporation commenced operating trams in 1901 with a fleet of open top four-wheel cars. In fact although the cars were replaced and rebuilt, it never operated any other type. The tram routes radiated from Old Steine, each route being assigned a letter that in most cases gave some indication of its destination, i.e. S for Station and E for Elm Grove. The trams were replaced in 1939 shortly before the outbreak of the Second World War by forty-four trolleybuses and twenty-one motor buses, all of AEC manufacture with bodies by Weymann. At the same time a co-ordination agreement was reached with Brighton Hove & District as described previously. The routes tended to follow those of the trams but were gradually extended to take account of new housing developments.

With extended services and increased traffic it became apparent that more vehicles were required. A further eight trolleybuses were acquired after the war, these having chassis by BUT, the organisation set up jointly by AEC and Leyland for the production of trolleybuses. Their Weymann bodies were similar to those on the 1939 AECs but with subtle differences that gave them a more modern appearance. A further fourteen motor buses arrived between 1947 and 1949, these being AEC Regent IIIs with handsome Weymann bodywork.

1959 saw the first stage of the trolleybus abandonment, motor buses replacing trolleybuses on all but the Hollingbury and Preston Drove services. The replacement buses were Leyland PD2s with Weymann bodies to the unattractive and basic Orion design. They were not favoured by the residents of the town who were quick to bemoan the loss of the silent, speedy trolleys. The second and final stages of the trolleybus abandonment took place on 30th June 1961. More Leyland PD2s were delivered, still with Orion-style Weymann bodies but of forward entrance layout of more pleasing appearance and officially named 'Aurora'. An interesting development was the purchase of four pre-war Leyland TD5s from Southdown as a stop-gap measure pending delivery of the final PD2s.

Brighton Corporation's biggest claim to fame was probably the introduction of the first one-man operated double-decker in Britain to run on normal stage carriage service. The bus concerned was one of the forward-entrance PD2s, which had had the front bulkhead window angled, leaving a space through which the driver could take money, give change and issue tickets. It was not exactly space-age technology but it worked extremely well; so well, in fact, that all thirty-five of the forward-entrance Titans were similarly adapted, allowing all but the busy 49/49A services to be converted to one-man operation.

Like Southdown and BH&D, Brighton Corporation remained faithful to the front-engined double-decker for as long as it could, the last being a batch of F-registered PD3s with Weymann bodies finished by Cammell-Laird of Anglesey. There followed a brief and unsuccessful flirtation with the rear-engined single-decker before the first Leyland Atlantean arrived in 1970, setting the trend for the rest of the decade.

Following the creation of the National Bus Company, Brighton Hove & District, now part of Southdown, had received some bad press largely due to staff and vehicle shortages. The Corporation decided to distance itself from BH&D by repainting its fleet blue and white, a move which proved to be unnecessary as almost immediately BH&D and Southdown buses began to appear in NBC leaf green and white!

To supplement the trolleybuses, Brighton Corporation took delivery of twenty-one motor buses at the same time. These were AEC Regent 0661s with 8.8 litre engines and Weymann 54-seat bodies very similar in appearance to the trolleys. Eleven of these buses had composite bodes and were fairly short-lived. The remaining ten, with metal-framed bodies, lasted well into the sixties. Working on a former trolleybus route, 63 is seen emerging from St James's Street which, incredible though it may seem today, was then a two-way thoroughfare. Having given a creditable 26 years' service to Brighton Corporation FUF 63 was purchased for preservation in 1965 and is happily still with us today. *Roy Marshall*

Just around the corner, sister bus 60 lays over at the anti-clockwise terminus of circular service 42. The restaurant on the corner, visible in both views, gave rise to the location being known as 'Lyon's Corner'. Behind number 60 is one of the elegant Weymann-bodied Regent IIIs delivered between 1947 and 1949. Although the picture was taken on 15th September 1964, more than three years after the introduction of the Brighton Area Transport Services agreement, Number 60 still carries its Brighton Hove & District Transport Fleetname. *Roy Marshall*

Between 1947 and 1950 Brighton Corporation put into service a further fourteen motor buses. They were AEC Regent IIIs with preselector gearboxes and handsome bodywork by Weymann. Their deep radiators with chromium surrounds and elegant Weymann bodywork made them classic buses and high on the list of enthusiasts' favourites. The Dyke Road tram route (H) was the only one not to be converted to trolleybus operation, the trams being replaced by two motor bus routes, service 51 via London Road and New England Road and 52 via the sea front and Brighton Station. These were worked initially by the original 1939 AEC Regent IIs and later by the Regent IIIs. One of the latter, number 89 is seen showing off its good looks at the Dyke Road terminus of service 51. The exception that proves the rule, it is showing 'Old Steine' as its destination rather than 'Aquarium'. *Howard Butler*

The Brighton trolleybuses were abandoned in two stages. The first in 1959 left only the 26/26A and 46/46A services remaining. For the first stage of the replacement, Brighton Corporation bought twenty Leyland PD2/37s with Weymann 61-seat bodies. But what a difference from the elegant Weymann bodies on the Regent IIIs with their handsome lines and Alhambrinal ceilings. These were to the current 'Orion' styling with unequal depth windows on each deck and a spartan interior. Not only were their interiors utilitarian but their hill-climbing ability could not begin to match that of the trolleys, and resulted in letters of complaint to the local press. Number 79 is seen climbing up to Higher Bevendean on its way to East Moulsecoomb. Services 49/49A were the Corporation's last crew-operated routes and were therefore the regular haunt of the 'back-loaders' during their final days. *Roger Knight*

For the final part of the abandonment Brighton Corporation bought a further fifteen PD2/37s again with Weymann bodies. This time, however, they were of forward entrance layout and somehow managed to look far more attractive than their rear-entrance brethren. The interiors were also less austere. Thirty of the type were taken into the fleet between 1961 and 1965 and all were eventually converted for pay-as-you-enter operation, in which guise they proved remarkably efficient. One, number 23, was the first to be so treated and was in fact the first one-man double-decker to operate in normal service in the UK. It is seen here in later days wearing the blue and white livery adopted in 1970. Once again the location is 'Lyon's Corner'. Brighton Corporation was always a great believer in maximising revenue from advertising and managed to fit no fewer than seventeen onto its front-entrance PD2s! *Dave Brown*

Brighton's epithet of 'Queen of Watering Places' is most apposite in this atmospheric shot taken in Old Steine during a cloudburst. Brighton Corporation PD2 number 8, displaying a particularly attractive pair of double front adverts for the Old Ship Hotel, splashes through the water on circular service 42. By the time this photo was taken, services 26/46 had been taken over by Brighton Hove & District in exchange for service 49 and the company's Bristol KSW6G 477 is seen on the left heading for Hollingbury on the 26B. On the right, one of the second batch of Southdown's convertible PD3s, 429 presents a one-eyed look with its offside opening vent having been donated to one of the 'panoramic' PD3s. *Roger Knight*

Brighton's final half-cabs were five late examples of the Leyland PD3/4 with Metro-Cammell bodies finished by Cammell Laird of Anglesey. Of basically similar outline to the PD2s, they were obviously longer, seating 69, and had a brighter interior colour scheme. Again they were all fitted for one-man operation. 34 is seen in Hartington Road passing under the railway bridge that carried the Kemp Town branch line. The line had been closed to passenger traffic in 1933 and was finally closed completely in 1971. The bridge was demolished in 1973. The 58 was normally operated by single-deckers and it is possible that the Marshall-bodied Panther Cub visible in the background has failed and been replaced by the PD3. *Roger Knight*

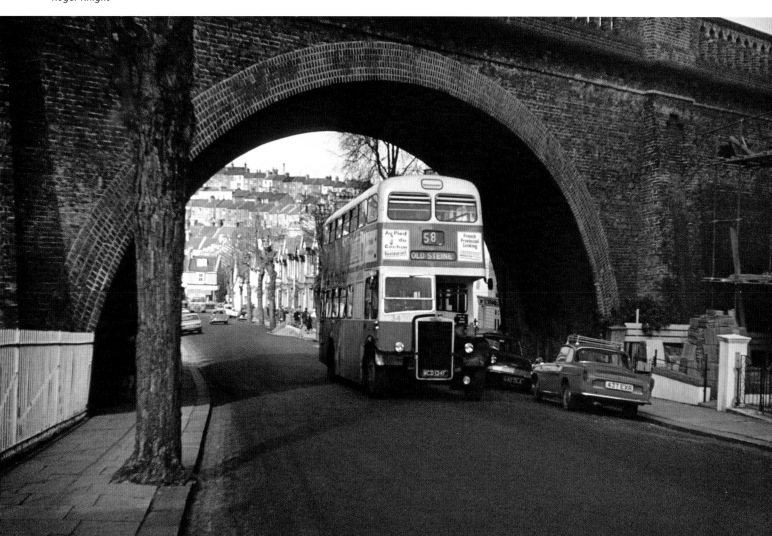

Left Although to much the same design as the PD2s, the PD3s had a far more upright rear end as can be seen in this view of 33 at Old Steine. They also had a large rear overhang that necessitated the rear lower panels being cut away for ground clearance. The one-man operated Titans usually showed 'Pay as you enter' on the rear destination screen – not the most appropriate place for it to be displayed! *Roger Knight*

Below left The late sixties was a time when rear-engined single-deckers were very much in vogue. Most operators tried them with varying degrees of success and Brighton Corporation was no exception. In 1968 it took delivery of seven Leyland Panther Cubs, three bodied by Strachan and the other four by Marshall. They were the first single-deckers in the fleet and, like most early rear-engined chassis, were not without mechanical problems, thus their stay was relatively short and all were withdrawn and sold in 1975. Both types are visible in this shot taken in Old Steine. In the centre is Marshall-bodied 39 on service 51, which together with the 52 were probably the routes to which they were most suited. On the left is number 36 with Strachan body which, in the opinion of the writer, was the more attractive of the two, working the 46A to Preston Drove. The 26A/46A 'inner circle' was a fairly quiet route on which these buses regularly performed although they were rarely seen on the 'outer circle' services to Hollingbury. On the right Southdown 369, one of the 'panoramic' PD3s, shows what happened to the opening vent from 429 shown on the previous page. *Roger Knight*

The first rear-engined double-deckers were also the first new vehicles to be delivered in the blue and white livery which, it has to be said, has a very clean, crisp look about it. The buses were Leyland Atlantean PDR1As with dual-door bodies by Willowbrook, a coachbuilder new to the operator. The photographer has managed to place number 82 neatly between the lamp post and the Keep Left sign as it speeds across the Race Hill with rolling Sussex countryside in the background. 82 was almost new when this shot was taken and is only just beginning to receive painted backgrounds for adverts! The area on the left between the two roads was used to set up a fairground for the film 'Oh What a Lovely War'. *Gerald Daniels*

EASTBOURNE CORPORATION

Eastbourne Corporation had the distinction of being the first municipal motor bus operator in Great Britain and possibly the world, its first service commencing in 1903. Unlike most municipal operators it never ran trams or trolleybuses but its motor buses had to fit in with the sedate character of the town. Prior to the Second World War all buses were petrol-engined so that the residents of the town should not be disturbed by the clatter of the diesel. The livery adopted was a rich blue, pale yellow and white; distinctive, striking and yet in keeping with the ambience of the town. For many years advertisements were painted in primrose directly on to the dark blue panels.

The fleet was made up largely of AECs and Leylands, fairly evenly divided, although other makes did creep in from time to time. In post-war years orders for bodywork went mainly to East Lancashire Coachbuilders although, again, there were exceptions.

As with the other operators covered in this volume, Eastbourne Corporation operated open-top buses on its sea front service. However, the beautiful and dramatic headland of Beachy Head to the west of the town was Southdown territory and the Corporation vehicles only travelled as far as the 'Foot of Beachy Head'. In later years a town tour was introduced using AEC Regent Vs with full drop windows and translucent roof panels. The Corporation and Southdown seemed to coexist quite amicably although unlike Brighton and Portsmouth there was never any formal agreement between the two concerns.

The 1960s was a time when operators were looking for any economies that could be made and in 1969 Eastbourne replaced its beautiful deep blue and primrose livery with an insipid all-over cream, a dark blue waistband and mudguards being the only relief. As was happening nation-wide, further savings were made by the introduction of one-man operation, initially using rear-engined single-deckers and later double-deckers of similar layout. Eastbourne never operated any forward entrance front-engined double-deckers.

One idiosyncrasy of the system was the clock at Eastbourne Station where conductors would dismount from their vehicles and set the hands of the clock to the time of the next departure. Another was that, until the most recent change in the registration system, on most vehicles the first digit of the registration number denoted the year the vehicle was new; thus KHC 370 was new in 1963. Eastbourne Corporation Motor Omnibus Department has also had the distinction of having a road in Eastbourne named 'Ecmod Road' in its honour.

Apart from a batch of Crossleys delivered in 1949, the double-deck fleet was made up fairly evenly of AECs and Leylands. Like many seaside operators Eastbourne converted a number of its older vehicles to open top for use on its sea front service. In 1949/50 four Leyland-bodied TD1s dating from 1932 had been converted to open top and, due to their colour, were given names starting with 'White'. They were withdrawn in 1953/4 and replaced by three TD4s and a TD5, again with Leyland bodies and similarly converted. Number 2 was the solitary TD5 dating from 1937. It was converted in 1956, some time after the TD4s. and given the name 'White Rose'. It was photographed at Eastbourne Pier in June 1962. *Omnicolour*

In 1939 Eastbourne took delivery of five Leyland Lion LT9 single-deckers with Leyland 32-seat bodies, but within two years four of the batch had been requisitioned by the Ministry of Defence. Number 12 remained in service until 1967 and survives in preservation to this day, being a familiar sight at rallies and running days in the south-east. For many years the residents of Eastbourne objected to the idea of having the peace and tranquillity of their town destroyed by the noisy diesel engine and therefore pre-war vehicles, the Lions included, were fitted with petrol engines. Number 12 eventually received the diesel engine from a withdrawn Southdown TS7 in 1954. It is seen passing Eastbourne Station closely followed by an East Lancs-bodied AEC Regent V. *Gerald Daniels*

Of the five Leyland Lions delivered to Eastbourne in August 1939, four were commandeered by the military during the Second World War, never to return to their seaside home. By way of compensation a further single-decker was purchased in 1950. This was an AEC Regal III with 7.7 litre engine and East Lancs 30-seat rear-entrance body. Classified as a dual-purpose vehicle it was closer to being a coach than a bus with some wonderful 'art deco' interior fittings. However, it did see service on stage carriage routes as well as private hire duties. The bus received the simplified pale cream and blue livery and was withdrawn in 1978, being sold to a private owner and kept for a while at the Castle Point Transport Museum, Canvey Island, being returned to its original deep blue and primrose livery. During this time it achieved a certain amount of stardom, appearing in two episodes of the BBC sitcom 'Hi-de'Hi'. It was re-purchased by Eastbourne Buses in 1992 and restored to full psv status, often being used in service when demand required. It remained in Eastbourne Buses' ownership until 2008 when it passed to Stagecoach with the sale of the company. Number 11 is seen here during its first spell of duty with Eastbourne Corporation outside the operator's original depot in Churchdale Road. *Alan Snatt*

In post-war years East Lancashire Coachbuilders became the usual supplier of bodywork, although a handful of AEC Regents was delivered in 1946/7 with handsome Weymann bodies as shown opposite. Also delivered in 1946/7 were six Leyland PD1s with East Lancs 52-seat bodies, the first Eastbourne buses to be fitted with diesel engines from new. Five of the six were converted to open-top, one of which was number 18 seen here passing Eastbourne Station on its way to the Foot of Beachy Head. *Roy Marshall*

The only one of the batch to escape conversion was number 15, which remained in original condition until its withdrawal in 1968. It is seen approaching Eastbourne Pier with a fine selection of British-built cars and commercials in the background. *Gerald Daniels*

Like Brighton, Eastbourne purchased AEC Regent IIIs with Weymann bodies in 1947, five in number. They were fitted with 7.7 litre engines as opposed to the 9.6 litre unit specified by Brighton and the interiors were less decorative but they were still very elegant vehicles. This view illustrates clearly Eastbourne's practice of applying advertisements in fleet livery colours, primrose and white applied directly onto the blue background. Eastbourne 20 was photographed at Eastbourne Station with, behind, one of the equally handsome Bruce-bodied Regent IIIs.
Roy Marshall

While Southdown tended to order their vehicles in dozens, Eastbourne frequently bought theirs in multiples of four and thus the 1948 intake consisted of four Leyland PD2/1s, four AEC Regent IIIs and eight Crossley DD42/5s. All had virtually identical bodies by East Lancs, although some were finished by Bruce Coach Works or its predecessor. Leyland PD2/1 number 26 for instance was finished by Air Dispatch of Cardiff, which was renamed Bruce Coach Works in September 1948, two months after this bus was delivered. It is seen passing Eastbourne Station with, on the right, AEC Regent number 70. *Omnicolour*

What were possibly Eastbourne's most handsome double-deckers arrived in 1951. These were AEC Regent IIIs with bodies by Bruce Coach Works of Cardiff built under licence to East Lancs. At the time these buses were delivered, Eastbourne Borough Council had just begun to issue three letter registration marks as shown by number 47 seen in Seaside. One might imagine that a thoroughfare with this name would be the seafront but this is not the case in Eastbourne, although the sea is not very far away. *Roy Marshall*

Eight of these elegant buses entered service with Eastbourne in 1950 and somehow managed to look so 'right' in the town. The handsome lines of number 48 are well displayed in this view. Once again we are fortunate in that one of these vehicles, number 42, has been preserved.
Gerald Daniels

From 1956 the standard Eastbourne double-decker was the AEC Regent V with bodywork as usual by East Lancashire Coachbuilders. Again, East Lancs managed to produce a very handsome-looking vehicle. Twenty-two were taken into stock between 1956 and 1963, all basically the same although there were minor differences between the four batches. Number 64 was one of the third batch delivered in 1962; until the introduction of the current vehicle registration system, it was customary on Eastbourne's buses for the first digit of the registration number to indicate the year of delivery. Delivered in traditional blue, primrose and white, the batch was repainted into pale cream with blue relief in 1968-69 and it is in this livery that 64 is seen here leaving Terminus Road for Old Town. *Roy Marshall*

67 was one of the final batch of five AEC Regent Vs of which no fewer than four survived into preservation, including this one. It is seen opposite Eastbourne Station wearing the beautiful rich blue, primrose and white livery and indeed it was the last Eastbourne vehicle so to do. Behind is one of the earlier Regent Vs in the insipid ivory and blue livery which replaced it. *Alan Snatt*

1966 saw a return to the Leyland PD2, this time with the not overly attractive St Helens front. Again they were fitted with bodies by East Lancs, but the design was more austere, lacking the graceful curves of the Regent Vs as can be seen from this shot of 77 at Eastbourne Station. These were the last vehicles to be delivered in the traditional blue and primrose and indeed the last new front-engined buses. 77 is actually still in existence being in use as a snack bar at a campsite in the Netherlands. *Gerald Daniels*

In 1966 a song by the Kinks reached the top five in the Hit Parade entitled 'Dedicated Follower of Fashion'. It related to fashions in clothing but it was also very true of the bus industry at the time. All over the country operators were buying rear-engined single-deckers and few were really successful. Eastbourne was no exception and in 1968 bought its first single-deckers for nearly thirty years. Three Daimler Roadliners with East Lancs bodies were received, which proved extremely troublesome and their lives with Eastbourne were short. Problems were encountered with the Cummins 9.6 litre engines and with the rubber suspension and the buses were unpopular with drivers and mechanics alike. In this view 90 was working on sea front service 6 to the Foot of Beachy Head and was photographed at Royal Parade. *Roy Marshall*

Also delivered in 1966 were three Leyland Panthers, to be followed by a further ten in 1970/71. These too had East Lancs bodies of dual door layout, another 'passing phase' that has since been abandoned almost everywhere outside London. Unlike the Roadliners they had a stepped waistline and unusual and somewhat old fashioned windows that did not help their appearance. Although not loved by Eastbourne, they outlasted the Roadliners and many subsequently spent several years further along the Sussex Coast working for the Bexhill Bus Company. Number 10, one of the second batch, passes Eastbourne Station on its way to Cherry Gardens on the western outskirts of the town. *Alan Snatt*

Unpopular they may have been but there is no doubting that Panther number 6 looks impressive in this view. Also shown to advantage is the equally impressive architecture of Eastbourne Station. *Alan Snatt*

Although things would change after privatisation, second-hand vehicles were a rarity in the Eastbourne Corporation fleet. However, in 1968 as well as the Panthers and Roadliners, the Corporation bought a Leyland Panther Cub with Strachan dual door body, very similar to those operated by Brighton Corporation. 90 had been a Leyland demonstrator and had in fact visited the town the previous year in that capacity. With Eastbourne demonstrating its claim to be one of the sunniest towns in Britain, the Panther Cub is seen in Beatty Road while working service 3. *John Bishop*

Eastbourne was even slower than its neighbours in adopting the rear-engined double-decker with its first examples not arriving until 1972. They were Leyland Atlanteans and hardly surprisingly had bodies by East Lancs, a combination of chassis and body manufacturer that had served the Corporation well since 1946. But now the rich blue and primrose had gone and the operator was demanding the exact fare from its passengers. Number 13 looked very bland and uninspiring in its off-white livery when photographed in Cornfield Road, Eastbourne. *John Bishop*